LINCOLN'S PHYSICIAN

a biography of Dr. William Smith Wallace

DONALD MOTIER

ISBN 978-1-959450-97-9 (softcover)
ISBN 978-1-959450-98-6 (ebook)

Printed in the United States of America.

Book Vine Press
2516 Highland Dr.
Palatine, IL 60067

For:
Dr. Wayne C. Temple and James Cornelius, Lincoln scholars par excellence and very good friends.

In memory of Sandy Temple.

For: Anela with all the love I could give.

BOOKS BY DONALD MOTIER

FICTION

Just Friends: A Novella and Two Short Stories (1984)
Just Friends, A Love Story (2003)
Unfinished Business (2003)
Return to Sónville (2005)
The Book of Joel (2005)
Saving C. J. (2020)

HISTORICAL FICTION

Mystic Chords of Memory: The Lost Journal of William Wallace Lincoln (2009)
Saving Lincoln: Mystic Chords of Memory Part 2 (2014)

BIOGRAPHY

Gerard: The Influence of Jack Kerouac's Brother on His Life and Writing (1991, 2010)
He Had Rare Lights: A Biography of William (Willie) Wallace Lincoln (2019)
The Waves: A Biography of Henry (Harry) Augustus Burnett, The Real Tiny Tim Cratchit and Little Paul Dombey (2021)

POETRY

Faces of Being (1971)
On the Hound and Other Prose-Poems 1970-78 (1978)
Mnemonicons: Prose Poems 1979–1990 (1991)
Co-Incidings: Collected Poems 1965–1991 (2001)
New Poems 2000–2008 (2009)

HISTORY/MEMOIR

Riverside: A History and Memoir (2017)

TRAVEL

On the Trak (2014–2015)
On the Hound (1978, revised with new material 2016)

EDITED BY DONALD MOTIER

The Gray Day and Other Poems by Charles P. Patton (2009)
The Collected Poems of Charles Penrose Patton 1962–1991 (2013)

ACKNOWLEDGMENTS

First and foremost, I want to thank Dr. Wayne C. Temple, retired Deputy Director of The Illinois State Archives and author of many books on Abraham Lincoln and his family and who graciously provided me with index cards detailing the life and activities of Dr. Wallace while living in Springfield and practicing medicine as the Lincoln family physician from 1836 till his death in 1867.

Also, Dr. Temple's article "Loafing With Lincoln" in the *Lincoln Herald,* Summer 1961, Vol. 63, No. 2, p 53–62, provided invaluable details.

Grateful acknowledgment is made to the staff at the following institutions:

Abraham Lincoln Presidential Library and Museum
University of Pennsylvania Archives & Record Center
Lancaster County History (formerly Lancaster County Historical Society)
and to Lincoln scholar James Cornelius.

CONTENTS

INTRODUCTION

I first became interested in Dr. William Smith Wallace while doing genealogical research for my historical novel ***Mystic Chords of Memory: The Lost Journal of William Wallace Lincoln*** *published in 2009. Family lore claimed that I was related to Mary (Todd) Lincoln through my 5th great-grandfather Revolutionary War General Andrew Christy Porter (September 24, 1743–September 18, 1813}) who is buried in Harrisburg Cemetery. He had two daughters, and one, Anne Maria, (Mary) Parker Porter (January 1, 1781–March 8, 1839) married my 4th great-grandfather Nicholas Boyd (1772–December 20, 1840). Both the Porter and Boyd families were neighboring landowners in southern Lancaster County Pennsylvania near Peach Bottom. General Porter's other daughter Elizabeth Rittenhouse Porter (September 27, 1769–June 21, 1850) married Robert Porter Parker (October 12,1760–March 4,1800). He was a founder of Lexington, Kentucky and Mary (Todd) Lincoln's grandfather. Mary (Todd) Lincoln is my 2nd cousin, 3x removed and Willie Lincoln is my 3rd cousin, 2x removed.*

*Further genealogical research on Ancestry.com revealed a possible family connection between the Wallace/Henderson families of East Earl, Lancaster County and the Powers/Henderson/Wallace families of Lancaster County. A brother of Dr. Wallace, Davies, married a Mary Ann Henderson. Their uncle was named Henderson Wallace, and a brother of my great-grandfather Sgt. Charles *Powers, Pennsylvania Volunteers Civil War veteran whose mother was Hannah Henderson was named Wallace Henderson Powers. This followed the 19th Century practice of giving children the last names of ancestors as first names. *Mary* Porter *Boyd had married Charles MacNair Powers.*

I had temporarily put thoughts of writing a biography of Dr. Wallace on the back-burner having written a sequel to ***Mystic Chords of Memory,***

Saving Lincoln *in 2014, a few unrelated works, and finally a biography of Willie Lincoln,* ***He Had Rare Lights*** *in 2019.*

While visiting Dr. Wayne C. Temple and his wife in Springfield, Illinois in June of 2021, Dr. Temple suggested writing a biography of Dr. Wallace that has never been done and I would be the perfect person to do it.

PART 1

THE WALLACE FAMILY OF EAST EARL, LANCASTER COUNTY, PENNSYLVANIA 1731–1802

"Robert Wallace came to America from Ireland in 1731 though he was by birth Scottish. He was born in Scotland in 1721 and died December 17, 1791 in East Earl, Lancaster County, Pennsylvania. He married Martha Davies, daughter of John and Elizabeth Anderson Davies on August 3, 1768. They had eight children: John, Josiah, Isaac, Elizabeth, William, Davies, and James and Thomas who were twins.

In 1761 Robert opened a *General Store on the property he built in East Earl, Lancaster County, Pennsylvania where his family had settled. The old homestead is one of the most handsome landmarks in the Eastern part of the county, built of limestone with walls of unusual thickness. Five generations of the Wallace family have been born there. The original part of the building was the center part of the present building with an addition attached to the west end in which was the store. When his family increased more room was needed. This part was raised two and a half stories and a roof was attached to the east end of the house.

Robert Wallace bequeathed the store to his son, John, John to his son Davies. Davies had four sons: Henderson Agnew, John Smith, William James,

Edward Davies and one daughter Mary Ann Wallace Falls, who all at different times ran the store.

John Wallace, son of Robert Wallace and Martha Davies Wallace was born June 23, 1769. He married Mrs. Lydia Smith daughter of Squire William Smith and Diana Edward Smith. They were married April 6, 1797 by Reverend Mr. Heith, an Episcopal clergyman of Churchtown, Pa.

The children of John and Lydia Smith Wallace were: Davies, born in 1798 and died in 1866. He married Mary Ann Henderson and resided in the old Wallace homestead and kept the store up to 1861 when they moved to Philadelphia where he held a position in the Naval office of the government.

The second child was Harriet born April 19, 1800. She never married and died September 8, 1878. Her father left her the farm now owned by Henry Decker. This tract of land included all the area in which the village of East Earl is now located (as of 1925). Harriet Wallace willed at her death part of the tract to George A. Wallace who founded the good-sized village that has been built around the Railroad Station and post office by that name. Much of this property is still in the Wallace name for the principal business of the locality is the coal, Lumber and feed establishment of Alan R. Wallace of this city.

The third child of this union was William Smith Wallace who was born August 10, 1802. Details of Dr. Wallace's life are contained throughout the text.

The fourth child, Mary Ann Wallace, married Cyrus Jacobs, an attorney at law of Lancaster May 1, 1828. They soon after moved to Burlngton, Iowa where Mr. Jacobs died in 1838. The widow Mrs. Jacobs married A. K. Fahnestock of Harrisburg. She died without leaving any children by either husband."

The fifth child was Robert Wallace who married Miss Martha Lenegan. In 1834 they moved to Green Village, Franklin County. Mrs. Wallace died when quite young and Mr. Wallace married Miss Jane Cresswell of Scotland, Franklin County. Robert Wallace was the father of ten children who are largely the ancestors of the many Wallace Families in Franklin County.

The sixth son of the Wallace family was John Price Wallace who moved to Franklin County in 1842.

The seventh was George Wallace who married Miss Jane McNiel of Pequea. They resided at East Earl all their lives. Mr. Wallace died in

1891 and Mrs. Wallace in 1896. He was the father of the late George A. Wallace and the grandfather of Alan B. Wallace.

Edward was the eighth son [born in 1807]. He became a physician, was a graduate of Princeton and *attended (like his older brother) The University of Pennsylvania Medical School. Dr. Edward Wallace began to practice medicine at Goodville. From there he went to Reading where he was one of the founders of Reading Hospital. He married one Miss Clara Haren of Connecticut. They had seven children. At the time of the Civil War he was for a time in the Navy. He died in 1872.

***The University of Pennsylvania Archives & Record Center, Selected List of Medical Students, 1805–1860, Surnames Beginning With "W" indicates he only attended the school year 1934–35 and did not graduate.**

Lydia Martha Wallace was the ninth and last child of this remarkable family. She married Colonel Nathaniel Kinzer of Blue Ball. In 1838 they followed the other Wallaces to Franklin County.

In the old graveyard around the Cedar Grove Church which is part of the original Wallace tract of land, lie the remains of more Wallace families than any other. Those who remained at or near the old Wallace homestead to the end of their lives are at rest in this Presbyterian God's acre. The tombstones contain the only history of many of them that can be found."

From: "The Wallace Family and the Wallace Store of East Earl," *Journal of the Lancaster County Historical Society,* Vol. 28, No. 2, 1925, no. 1."

According to a young librarian friend of mine who happens to be from East Earl, the general store is now a Dollar Tree. He added he is very familiar with the Wallace and Diller families of that area having grown up there.

PART 2

WILLIAM SMITH WALLACE'S CHILDHOOD 1802–1821

William Smith Wallace worked at the family general store when not in school until leaving for Philadelphia to study medicine at the University of Pennsylvania Medical school In September 1821 at age 19.

PART 3

ATTENDS UNIVERSITY OF PENNSYLVANIA MEDICAL SCHOOL 1822–1823

According to the *University of Pennsylvania Archives & Record Center, Selected Lists of Medical Students, 1805–1860, Medical Department Matriculants, 1806–1852 Surnames Beginning with "W" indicates that William S. Wallace attended the Medical School for the years 1821–22 and 1822–23 but did not graduate as there is no "$" symbol after his name in the key on the introductory page.

However, according to Records of the Medical Alumni Society, University of Pennsylvania, courtesy of a Mr. R. Houston, obtained by Dr. Wayne C. Temple, William Smith Wallace graduated in 1824.

Historian Stephen Berry in his book *House of Abraham: Lincoln and the Todds, a*lso states that Wallace graduated from medical school in 1824. I contacted him at his office at the University of Georgia inquiring about his source but he never got back me.

I'm inclined to trust the University Archives.

*See photocopies after photographs.

PART 4

PRACTICES MEDICINE IN LANCASTER, PENNSYLVANIA 1824–1836

After attending medical school Wallace returned to East Earl until he started a medical practice Lancaster County but soon lost interest in that field after developing the idea of land speculating in the Midwest and left sometime in 1835.

In an interview with Frances Todd Wallace in the *Chicago Times-Herald* of August 25, 1895 she states that after an unsuccessful venture in Iowa at the suggestion of *Pennsylvania friends, he stopped in Springfield, Illinois.

*Possibly Dillers.

PART 5

LEAVES LANCASTER IN 1836 TO TRY LAND SPECULATING IN THE MIDWEST, SETTLES IN SPRINGFIELD, ILLINOIS. OPENS MEDICAL PRACTICE/DRUGSTORE IN 1837

"Practically all of the Wallaces of the older generations were storekeepers for at least a portion of their lives. They were all astute businessmen whose word was as good as their bond and who dealt only in the best commodities available.

But alas it was not so destined that all the Wallaces should follow the family tradition. Or, perhaps that's not quite the fact. Maybe it was the original strain of the original Robert Wallace that sent his grandson, Dr. William Smith Wallace into the remote frontiers of the middle west away from calico and yardsticks. Maybe it was that strain of adventure that sent the first Wallace against the peddlers which urged Dr. Wallace to stumble into the piquant romance of the great Lincoln.

At any rate he chose to give up his practice in the family habitat, East Earl, and go west to the prairies of Illinois [and Iowa]."

The Sundays News, Lancaster, Pennsylvania, Sunday August 14, 1932, p.13, H. Clifton Thorbahn, "History of the Wallace Clan: Robert Wallace Opened A General Store in East Earl Twp."

Not wanting to continue his medical practice in Lancaster in May of 1836 he left to try land speculating in the Midwest. That failed, and on his way back from Iowa stopped in Springfield, Illinois and some men from Pennsylvania [possibly Dillers] who had accompanied him urged him to settle there which he did opening a medical practice in 1837.

The **Sangamo Journal* of Springfield reported that Dr. Wallace was offering "his services to the inhabitants of Springfield and vicinity. He may be found at his drugstore; the Golden Mortar, No. 4, street level, in Hoffman's Row." As it happens, Wallace's drugstore was just downstairs from Lincoln's Law Office. Lincoln did not smoke or use tobacco, but he often hung around those who did, while they did, to ply them with good stories and good jokes he would become famous for. Wallace was a captive audience for such things. *It was founded by Josiah Francis and the first issue was November 10, 1831. It lasted till 1847 when it became the *Illinois Daily Journal.*

Dr. Wallace bought the drugstore of A. W. Hughes who had come to Springfield from Baltimore and opened it on July 2, 1836 but after a year sold it to Dr. Wallace. Hughes returned east and died in 1878 at Washington, D. C. Having difficulty balancing a growing medical practice and running a general store, Dr. Wallace hired Jonathan Roland Diller, Esq. (1814–June 27, 1849) and operated the drugstore until the partnership was mutually dissolved on April 12, 1849. The drugstore sold drugs, medicines, paints, oils, dye, snuffs and cigars and a tonic for fever and ague bitters according the July 28–29 issue of the *Sangamo Journal.* The first ad of the store appeared on September 23, 1837 in the *Sangamo Journal.* Diller was 23 and Wallace 35 at the time.

Mr. Diller was also a member of the Diller family that had a farm in the East Earl area of Lancaster County and they and the Wallace families had been friends for generations. Mr. Diller had arrived in Springfield from Lancaster in 1837 according the *Springfield Gazette.* Mr. Diller died of "hemorrhage of the lungs" on June 27, 1849. He had also been Postmaster of Springfield.

On November 11, 1844 Wallace & Diller started running a notice in the *Sangamo Journal* that they were located on the east side of the public square.

OBITUARY OF ROLAND WEAVER DILLER.

ROLAND WEAVER DILLER, pioneer settler of Illinois and an intimate friend of Abraham Lincoln died yesterday (August 18, 1905) at Springfield, Illinois of a lingering illness at the age of 85 years. One son [Isaac Roland Diller II. July 14, 1854–September 28, 1943] and two daughters survive him.

In 1844 another member of the Diller family, Roland Weaver Diller (October 15, 1822–August 18, 1905), a cousin of the late Jonathan Roland Diller, was born in Downingtown Chester County, Pennsylvania which borders Lancaster County came to Springfield. He established a partnership with Charles Sharpless Corneau in the drug [store] business in 1849 and upon the death of Mr. Corneau became sole proprietor of the store which he continued until a few years ago when he retired from active pursuits.

The drugstore was one of the landmarks of the city located in the heart of the business district. Mr. Diller ignored the progress of time and kept in his store the same furniture and fittings it held when it was the political headquarters for both great political parties in Illinois.

Abraham Lincoln and Stephen A. Douglas, as well as all the other leaders of a half-century ago were numbered among the intimate friends of Mr. Diller who has been a fruitful source of information to biographers of these great publicists.

In 1878 Roland's son, *ISAAC ROLAND DILLER (II) [July 14, 1854–September 28, 1943] joined his father in the operation of the store. As a young boy, Isaac was a playmate of Willie and Tad and there is a photo of him in front of the Lincoln home. Isaac Roland Diller spent his whole life in Springfield with the exception of a few years when he was away at school. He was born July 14, 1854, son of Roland Weaver Diller and Esther *Coates (Ridgeway) Diller. The early education of Isaac was acquired I n the Springfield public school along with Willie Lincoln (and Tad sporadically) and he graduated from high school in 1871. He attended the Chicago College of Pharmacy 1873–74 and graduated from the Philadelphia College of Pharmacy in the Centennial Class of 1876. He entered his father's drug store in 1878 and followed that business until 1901 with the exception of two years devoted to Y. M. C. A. work.

He had been connected with the local branch of the Association since he helped organize it in 1874 and was always most actively interested in the good work. In 1907 he became engaged in the business of Real estate, Mortgage Loans and Insurance.

*Coates, she was a member of the founding family of Coatesville, Chester County, Pennsylvania.

Mr. Diller was married in Springfield June 30, 1880 to Addie May Hughes who was born in Springfield February 19, 1856, daughter of William Thompson and Dorinda (Scott) Hughes. Mr. Diller and his wife had one son, William Hughes Diller born February 26, 1884. Mr. Diller united with the Presbyterian Church in 1866. He was reared a Democrat but in 1885 he became identified with the Prohibition Party and for several years served as County and City Secretary of that party. Mr. Diller was active in furthering the best interests and moral welfare of his community and had many warm friends in his work. His earnestness and singleness of purpose was universally recognized and was highly esteemed for this many excellent qualities of mind and heart.

He possessed an inexhaustible fund of anecdotes relating to these two and the other leaders of early Illinois and never tired of relating them. Mr. Diller was active in the affairs of the Old Settlers Association of Sangamon County from its organization in 1894. He was three-times president of the society and his election to the office of secretary followed, holding this office for a quarter of a century. On September 28, 1943 at the ripe old age of 89 Mr. Diller died in Springfield. He is buried in Oak Ridge Cemetery, Plot, 10,47. From the *Illinois State Journal,* August 18, 1905 and *Findagrave.com* March 31, 2022.

*"Much confusion has resulted from the fact that there were two men by the name of Isaac Roland Diller living in Springfield. To keep the record straight I [Dr. Wayne C. Temple] have identified Roland Weaver Diller's son as being Isaac Roland Diller II. The other man I have called Isaac Roland Diller I. He was a brother of Isaac Roland Diller and was born in Downingtown, Pennsylvania in *1818."—Dr. Wayne C. Temple.

*According to *The Diller Family* by J. L. Ringwalt, privately printed, Philadelphia, 1878, Isaac R. Diller was born in 1819 in Lancaster County, Pennsylvania and died November 18, 1891 age 71–72. There was another Isaac Diller born in Lancaster County in 1818 but he had a different brother from Roland. *Actually, the name Isaac Diller was common in the Lancaster/Chester County region of Pennsylvania in the 19th century.

ISAAC ROLAND DILLER, 1819–November 18, 1891, brother of Roland Weaver Diller.

Isaac Roland Diller was born in Lancaster County, moved with his parents to Downingtown, Chester County and was apprenticed to a West Chester printer. He was a close friend of Bayard Taylor [January 11, 1825–December 19, 1878]. Both became prominent in many fields Taylor was a noted novelist, and always remained close friends. After finishing his apprenticeship, he became joint proprietor of the *Citizen-Soldier* in Philadelphia and later occupied a similar position in Harrisburg.

On the breaking out of the Mexican War, he enlisted in the First Pennsylvania Regiment, was made Commissary with the rank of Captain, a title he carried throughout life. He accompanied General Scott to Mexico City. After being discharged he came to Springfield where his sister Maria and brother Roland lived. He was elected Reading Clerk in the House of Representatives of the Illinois Legislature, entered the real estate business. He was appointed Postmaster under President Pierce. He took a prominent part in Masonry and was State Orator and also Chairman of the Illinois State Democratic Committee, which brought him in close fellowship with Stephen A. Douglas. In 1852 he married Lenora Heaton and built a fine home in Springfield that was torn down only in 1940. However, property interests in Chicago took him there to live and there he continued in the real estate business. He was the United States consul to Bremen, Germany under President Buchanan and also to Florence, Italy under President Cleveland. He died in Philadelphia on November 18, 1891, aged 71–72.

At the time of his death he was buried in Oak Ridge Cemetery, Springfield. His remains were removed to Chicago October 1895. Location of that cemetery is unknown, but it is probably Rosehill in Chicago. His wife, who later died in Evanston, now lies beside him. Being childless, they adopted a daughter, Linda who is also buried by them. *IBID, the Diller Family*, by J. L. Ringwalt.

PART 6

MARRIES MARY (TODD) LINCOLN'S SISTER IN 1839 AND LATER BECOMES LINCOLN FAMILY PHYSICIAN

The *Sangamo Journal,* May 24, 1839, recorded the following "MARRIED—IN THIS TOWN at the residence of N. W. Edwards, Esq., on Tuesday evening [May 21, 1839} by the Rev. Mr. Charles Dresser, WILLIAM S. WALLACE. M.D. to Miss FRANCES J., daughter of Robert S. Todd, Esq. of Lexington, KY."

Also, listed: *Marriage Record,* II, 89, Courthouse, Sangamon County, Springfield, Illinois.

In an interview in the *Chicago Sunday Times-Herald* of August 25, 1895, Frances (Todd) Wallace (March 7, 1817–August 14, 1899) stated "she got acquainted with Dr. Wallace and he and I kept company quite a while and then we were married"

The couple was married at the home of Elizabeth Todd Edwards (November 13, 1813–February 22, 1888), Frances' sister on May 21, 1839. Mary Todd then moved back to Springfield where Lincoln had lived since 1837. The Wallaces started married life by living at Springfield's Globe Tavern in the very same room that the Lincolns would later occupy for four dollars a week. Dr. Wallace later recalled, "Mr. L, before he was married used to come to our house—was attached to my eldest girl." (Mary J. Wallace 1842–1911 married Col. John P, Baker November 15, 1865).

The Wallaces had five children:

Elizabeth, died in infancy
Mary J. Wallace Baker (1842–1911)
William Fonday Wallace (1845–1923)
Frances Wallace (1848–1881)
Charles Edwards Wallace (1858–1874)

St. Paul's Episcopal Church Parish Register, II, 118, 1838–1905, lists the following children of William and Frances Wallace baptized in a private service November 18, 1849:

Mary Jacobs Wallace
William Fonday Wallace
Frances Wallace

Elizabeth Todd Grimsley remarked that William Smith Wallace was a 'portly gentleman.'

Elizabeth Todd Grimsley, "Six Months In The White House," *Journal of The Illinois State Historical Society.* October 1926–January 1927.

"It turned out when Mary Todd married Abraham Lincoln in preference to Stephen A. Douglas Her decision was the result of repeated urging on the part of her brother-in-law Dr. Wallace.

Mary Todd was at the time twenty-two years old; plump, swift, beaming with ready answers slipping from a sharp tongue it was told. She had her gifts, a smooth soft skin, soft brown hair and flashing blue eyes. With her somewhat short figure sheathed in a gown with white with black stripes cut low at the neck and her skirt fluffed out in a slightly baloonish hoop shod in modish ballroom slippers, she was the center of likes and dislikes among those who visited the Edwards mansion where she was a guest of her sister Elizabeth wife of Ninian W. Edwards.

Lincoln could keep his head and outguess lights, shoals and sandbars on the Ohio and Mississippi rivers and take flatboats through, but with Mary Todd he lost his head. His experience was rich rivers, starved with women as one woman remarked, He didn't go as much as other young men for ladies' company.'

Dr. Wallace watched the budding romance. He knew Mary Todd; he knew Abraham Lincoln. He also knew Stephen A. Douglas. Then, as the affair progressed, he studied all three of the participants cooly, as became a medical man who was interested not only from a medical standpoint but from a romantic standpoint as well.

During her first year in Springfield both Abraham Lincoln and Stephen A. Douglas took their turns being entertained by Mary Todd in the big parlor of the Edwards house, took turns escorting her to parties and balls. She was asked which of the two she intended to have as her husband and answered, "'The one that had the most chance at being president.'"

As the months went by and she found herself unable to choose between the two men, her vitality was sapped and so undermined that she became ill.

Dr. Wallace was called and diagnosed her trouble and told her frankly that she was in a state of indecision. He advised her to drop Douglas and accept Lincoln as Lincoln's habits were better than Douglas' and he had a better prospect for a career than Douglas had. She obeyed this medical injunction and became Mrs. Lincoln."

The Sunday News, Lancaster, Pennsylvania, August 14, 1932, p. 13, H. Clifton

Thornbahn, "History of the Wallace Clan: Robert Wallace Opened A General Store in East Earl. Twp."

PART 7

LINCOLN'S THIRD SON WILLIAM "WILLIE" WALLACE LINCOLN BORN DECEMBER 21, 1850 AND NAMED FOR DR. WALLACE

Willie tragically died of smallpox and typhoid on February 20, 1862 at age eleven. Lincoln was devastated as Willie was his favorite. Willie was most like his father in temperament, empathy and intelligence, already writing poems and little political speeches.

PART 8

DR. WALLACE'S PROFESSIONAL AND POLITICAL ACTIVITIES 1838–1860

The following two articles are from the *Sangamo Journal:*

> Among those appointed to a committee on September 8, 1838 for a Whig barbecue to celebrate the election of John Todd Stuart to Congress was Dr. Wm. S. Wallace.
>
> On January 26, 1839 at a meeting of the Whig Young Men of Springfield and Sangamon County held at the Courthouse, Dr. Wallace was put on the committee of 15 to address the Whig Young Men.
>
> "Lincoln got well acquainted with Wallace's partner (Jonathan Diller) and liked him very much. Both men (Lincoln and Diller served as managers of the cotillion party which was held at the American House on December 16, 1839. Later, on December 17, 1844, Lincoln wrote to John J. Hardin [January 6, 1810-February 23, 1847] (the local Congressman) and asked that Jonathan Roland Diller be appointed postmaster of Springfield. Diller appointed Postmaster

at Springfield received the political plum. And when Diller asked for more money, Congressman Lincoln took time to reply from Washington on January 19, 1848. Bur most of the Dillers were Democrats and Jonathan was no exception. Although Lincoln, a Whig, had befriended him, Diller continued to delve deeper into Democratic politics. Finally, on April 7, 1849, Lincoln wrote to the Postmaster General and declared that he wished Abner Y. Ellis at Springfield. "'J. R. Diller, the present incumbent, I cannot say he has failed in his proper discharge of any of the duties of the office,"' Lincoln reported, "'He however,'" Lincoln explained, "'has been an active partisan in opposition to us. Located at the Seat of Government he has been, for part, if not the whole of the time he has held the office, a member of the Democratic State Central Committee…'" "As a result of this letter Diller got the ax and Ellis became Postmaster. Ellis had formerly been the partner of Joshua Fry Speed [November 14, 1814–May 29, 1892] (Lincoln's most intimate friend) in the firm of Abner Y. Ellis [November 30, 1807–March 10, 1872] and Company. One wonders how much assistance J. R. Diller had rendered Dr. Wallace in the store. Perhaps Diller had only supervised the post office and spent most of his time selling drugs, but it is more likely that he was completely occupied with the problems of the United States Mail. There is only one other explanation: Diller most have furnished a large amount of capital. For some reason the firm of Wallace and Diller was dissolved five days after Lincoln recommended Diller's removal from the post-mastership." *Lincoln Herald*, Summer 1961, Vol. 63, No. 2, Wayne C. Temple, "Loafing With Lincoln", p 56.

At a meeting of surgeons and physicians of Illinois at Springfield on June 9, 1840, Dr. Wallace was put on the committee to make arrangements.

William H. Herndon (1819–1891) and Dr. Wm. S. Wallace were members of the Sangamon County Whig Committee. S*angamo Jour*n*a*l, February 15, 1844.

Dr. William S. Wallace was to be appointed Pension Agent at Springfield, Illinois on June 30, 1849. Lincoln got him the job. He was to replace Charles R. Hurst who had resigned. This was from the *Illinois Daily Journal,* June 11, 1849.

The following articles are from the *Illinois Daily Journal:*

The Mayor and Aldermen of Springfield appointed a three-man Board of Health for the city of Springfield. Dr. Anson G. Henry (October 3, 1804–July 30, 1865) and Dr. William S. Wallace were two of the members. This City Board of Health was to recommend a system of measures to the Board for the cleansing of the city—if he should deem such a measure necessary. The Board was to meet at Dr. Walllace's office on March 30, 1849.

Dr. Wm. S. Wallace was named on a committee to meet at the Supreme Court Room in Springfield on June 2, 1849 to form a Horticultural Society. Also, on the committee were John Todd Stuart, Ninian W. Edwards (April 15, 1809–September 2, 1889), Dr. John Todd (April 27, 1787–January 7, 1865), etc. June 1, 1849.

The Board of Health for Springfield met at the Mayor's Office on July 18, 1849. Dr. John Todd, Dr. Meredith Helm (March 2, 1802–March 9, 1866), Dr. Gershom Jay ne (October 15, 1791–April 17, 1867), Wm. S. Wallace, and A. G. Henry were present. Dr. Todd was elected president and Dr. Helm secretary. They warned the citizens to be prepared for an outbreak of the Asiatic cholera, warned the town to keep the streets clean, watch their diet, establish temporary hospitals, get their medicine at local druggists, form nursing homes, keep plenty of ventilation rooms, keep strangers out of town because of crowding due to lack of housing. July 23, 1849.

OBITUARY OF JOHN ATHAN ROLAND DILLER JUNE 27, 1849

From the *Springfield Gazette*

In this city on the 27th day of June of hemorrhage of the lungs Jonathan Roland Diller, Esq. Late Postmaster of this city in the 35th year of his age. It is always a duty at once painful and sorrowful to record The death our citizens and neighbors but it becomes particularly poignant when in this instance the dispensation of Providence touches the cords of sincere friendship, the most devoted attachment awakes the keenest sensibilities and open the fountain of uncontrollable grief. In the death of Diller we have lost one of our best and upright citizens—society an ornament and his associates a sincere and true friend. For the last twelve years he has been a resident in our midst. He came here proudly and honorably recommended of his native county (Lancaster, PA.) and it were useless for us here in the midst of such friendships and affections as centered about him to say how he has redeemed nobly and manfully the pledges of the friends of his youth. Engaged for some eight years in the drug business in connection with Dr. Wallace all of our citizens have cause to remember with what care industry and universal politeness and skill he discharged his duty in this difficult and responsible profession. So great was his popularity and so great was the esteem of the people that when four years since he received from Mr. Polk the post-mastership of this city, the appointment was hailed with one universal burst of appreciation from all classes of our citizens. Of the manner in which he conducted the business of the post office it is only necessary to reiterate the language of the *Daily Journal*, "there never was a better public officer."

In politics he was a firm unyielding Democrat and this added to the fact that his health had suffered very severely by close and unremitted application to the duties of his office induced him to write out his resignation much against the wishes of the community who strongly insisted his remaining in office. His removal in May, however, obviated the necessity of resignation and relieved of the responsibilities of his office his friends looked to a renewal of his usual health and buoyancy of spirits. But alas the wily and insidious foe was busy at his heartstrings but after a partial confinement of a few weeks he was attacked with hemorrhage of the lungs and although frequently stayed in the fearful ravages of the medical skill of his physicians it had taken too deep a hold to be eradicated and nature at length sunk under the repeated attacks.

The deep heart of our community is shrouded in mourning and the silent grief of the people attests to the sincerity of their friendship and the respect paid to his memory. The place he occupied in our

> midst is now vacant and oh how hard it will go for us to fill it for:
>
> "None that knew him need be told, a warmer heart death ne'er made cold."

To his relatives here and in Pennsylvania we can but offer the oil of consolation and the incense of pure and holy sympathy in this their day of sorrow and night and affliction and we entreat them to be reminded that beyond the darkness of the tomb arises a holier a purer day bright with promises and brilliant with hope and to that glorious future the sorrowing, the heart-broken and the heavy-laden must look for shelter and comfort and consolation when the day goeth dawn in sorrow and the night is full of grief.

*I included the full, flowery text of the obituary as an example of the journalistic English of the times. A shorter obituary appeared in the *Illinois State Journal,* June 29, 1849

When Dr. William S. Wallace was Pension Agent in Springfield, his office was over (Stacy B.) Opdycke (January 1, 1795–June 9, 1858) and (William Bradford) Fonday's (May 14, 1821–February 19th, 1862) Store. This was his Pension Agent Office—not his M.D. office which was at Corneau (Charles Sharpless January 16, 1826–January 9, 1860) and Diller's Drugstore. The Lincoln family bought cough candy, castor oil and hair balsam there. September 5, 1849. Seth M. Tinsley (August 8, 1808–1870) also operated a business at this time.

The following two articles are from the *Illinois Daily Journal*:

> Dr. Wm. S. Wallace was listed as the examining physician for the Connecticut Mutual Life Insurance Company of Hartford, Connecticut. [note that Charles M. Smith, a cousin from Lancaster had one of these positions at his death]. July 23, 1850.
>
> Dr. Wallace arrived home on Thursday [June 29, 1854] evening from his visit to see Eastern friends, in good health. June 30, 1854.

> The *Springfield Directory 1855–56* lists Dr. Wallace's house as being on the corner of Market and 7th Street. 1855.

In an article from the *Journal of the Illinois State Historical Society, XLVII, 57–58 (Spring 1954)* "Recollections of a Springfield Doctor," stated on May 1, 1857 Dr. Preston H. Bailhache (February 21, 1835–October 28, 1919) became a partner of Dr. William Smith Wallace in practice of medicine. Their office was over Johnson & Bradford's Bookstore on the southwest corner of the public square. Dr. Wallace would also see patients at his residence on the corner of 7th and Market Streets. Also see same article May 1, 1857 issue of the *Illinois Daily Journal.*

The Illinois State Journal reported on May *24, 1857 that* Dr. William Smith Wallace was a member of the Protestant Episcopal Church in Springfield.

The following three articles are from the *Illinois State Journal:*

> By April 23, 1859, Dr. Preston H. Bailhache had left Springfield for the gold fields and the *Journal* designated him their official correspondent. April 23, 30 1859.
>
> Dr. Preston H. Bailhache, the partner of Dr. William S. Wallace was back in Springfield on October 8, 1859 after being in the Pikes Peak Gold Fields. October 10, 1859.
>
> Wallace & Bailhache's ad by October 18, 1859 announced that their office is in the Smith, Wickersham Co. Building on the west side of the public square. Dr. Wallace also had an office at Corneau & Diller's Drugstore.
>
> Dr. Preston H. Bailhache was the First Assistant Surgeon, 19th Illinois Infantry Regiment commissioned July 16, 1861. On February 16, 1863, Dr. Bailhache became the Surgeon of the 14th Illinois Cavalry Regiment, mustered in on March 2, 1863; mustered out on July 31, 1865. *Report Adjutant General State of Illinois, II, 118, VIII, 453.*

The following two articles are from *Lincoln Talks,* Isaac R. Diller in Emanuel Hertz., N.Y., 1939, 74–75.

> When the store of Wallace & Diller early became the visiting place of Mr. Lincoln, for Mr. Wallace was his brother-in-law. When the firm subsequently changed, its drug store continued to be Mr. Lincoln's headquarters when he went downtown and did not go to his office. I remember when the store was burning meeting Mr. Lincoln with an armful of bottles he was trying to save. He stubbed his toe near the door and dropped all the bottles. He said he was no good as a bottle carrier and left the building. He returned, however, to help carry out the stove. October 18, 1859.
>
> When the new store was built to replace the one burned in 1858, Lincoln continued to sit around the stove there. Dr. Wallace liked Lincoln's stories but could never get the punchline correct. Lincoln used old stories but changed them to fit circumstances which he wanted to point out. Talk around the store generally turned to politics, IBID, p. 75.
>
> As Dr. Wayne Temple said, "It became Lincoln's loafing spot."
>
> Dr. Wallace's home in 1860 was at 81 South 7th Street at the corner of 7th and Market (now called Capitol). This was on the east side of 7th. Springfield City Directory 1860-61.
>
> The Springfield Census of 1860 lists that Dr. William S. Wallace was 56, a physician, had $10,000 in real estate roughly equal to $400,000 in 2022 values and had $1,000 in personal estate and had been born in Pennsylvania. *Census of 1860,* Illinois State Archives.

PART 9

DR. WALLACE ACCOMPANIES LINCOLN TO WASHINGTON AND WALLACE'S CIVIL WAR SERVICE 1861–1866

Dr. William Smith Wallace accompanied Lincoln when he left Springfield, Illinois bound for the nation's capital on February 11, 1861.

New York Tribune, February 12, 1861.

> "I hope you will give Dr. Wallace some good appointment... I believe I have said enough to explain my feeling on that subject."
>
> John T. Stuart to A. Lincoln, Springfield, April 3, 1861, in David C Mearns, ed., *The Lincoln Papers*, N.Y., 1948, II, 519.
>
> Dr. Wallace writes to Lincoln in order to plead for an office for his brother Edward. Says his relationship to the president has hurt his chances for a job. William S. Wallace to A. Lincoln, Springfield, Illinois, April 11, 1861, Robert Todd Lincoln Collection.
>
> Dr. Edward Wallace [1807–1872], brother of William S. Wallace, was appointed Naval Officer for

the Port of Philadelphia by Lincoln's decision. It paid $5,000 per year. *U. S. Official Register 1861, 62.*

Dr. Edward Wallace was a graduate of Princeton and [attended] University of Pennsylvania Medical School. He began his practice in Goodville. From there he went to Reading [Berks County, PA.], where he was one of the founders of the Reading Hospital. He married Miss Clara Haren of Connecticut. They had seven children. *Journal of the Lancaster County Historical Society*, Spring, Vol. 28, no. 2, 1925, "The Wallaces and the Wallace Store of East Earl"," p.4

"Dr. Wallace (William Smith), you know is needy, and looks to me; and I personally owe him much." A. Lincoln to John T. Stuart, Washington, March 30, 1861, Basler, ed., *Collected Works,* IV, 303.

Dr. Wallace got his appointment by Lincoln's influence and he in turn was influenced by his wife, Mary (Todd) Lincoln. Mary Lincoln wrote that Frances Wallace "little knows what a hard battle I had for it and how near he came to getting nothing."

Dr. William Smith Wallace was appointed Paymaster with the rank of Major on May 15, 1861. *Report, Adjutant General State of Illinois at* the time of the Civil War, Springfield, 1886, I, 175.

Part of the time Dr. Wallace served in Springfield, Illinois, then in Dept. of the Missouri the remainder of his time at the front along the lower Mississippi. His nephew, Edward D. Wallace of East Earl, was on his staff as Captain.

According to Frances (Todd) Wallace was at first stationed in Washington but "asked to be sent closer to home and was sent to St. Louis for a while.

Chicago Sunday Times-Herald, "Interview with Frances (Todd) Walllace," August 25, 1895.

While Dr. William Wallace was serving in Mississippi he contracted some debilitating disease [probably dysentery]. A doctor treating Wallace sent a letter describing his urinary tract problems to Dr. Edward Wallace, who forwarded it to President Lincoln in early March 1865. "Your brother Major Wallace for the last week or ten days has been more comfortable, has had less hectic or none at all, and very much less supperation from his fistulous openings. His appetite is good for a man lying still and his digestion good. He still passes water with some spasmodic action about the neck of the bladder and at nearly all times with some little dribbling through the fistulas—yet he passes water without going through any of the artificial openings."

Preston H. Bailhache, "Recollections of a Springfield Doctor," *Journal of the Illinois State Historical Society*, Volume 49, (1954), p.59.

On March 7, 1866, Major William Smith Wallace retired from active service. He was allowed proper pay but was subject to assignment to duty as the President might direct. Service record of W. S. Wallace, National Archives, Washington, D.C.

U.S. Civil War Soldier Record and Profiles 1861–1865, Index To Compiled Military Service Records, Heitman Register of United States Army 1789–1903.

William S. Wallace enlisted and was mustered in May 15, 1861 as a Major in the Regular Army Paymaster Dept. by commission. He was mustered out May 7, 1866.

PART 10

ILLNESS AND DEATH OF DR. WALLACE

OBITUARIES OF DR. WILLIAM S. WALLACE:

ANOTHER OLD CITIZEN GONE—Died in this city on the morning of the 23rd of May, 1867. Dr. William S. Wallace, in the 66th year of his age.

In the death of Dr. Wallace, the city has lost a useful member; a man above suspicion of this world; a man of genial and social disposition; one who loved all and was beloved by all who knew him. As a physician his judgment was seldom erroneous. He was usually prompt in attending to the calls of professional duty and was ever kind and sympathetic in the sick room.

Dr. Wallace was a native of the city of Lancaster [actually of East Earl in the county] Pennsylvania. [and attended The University of Pennsylvania Medical School NOT Jefferson Medical College]. He commenced the practice of medicine in this city and attained a remarkable degree of success and popularity in his profession.

On May 21, 1839 he was married to Miss Frances J. Todd, a most amiable, lovely lady who still lives to lament his loss. Dr. Wallace served a term as pension agent under an appointment from President Taylor and also filled other important offices of trust.

In 1861 he was appointed a paymaster of the United States Army, a position he held at the time of his death. *Illinois State Register,* May 24, 1867

Dr. Wallace died at 1 a. m. on May 23, 1867 at his residence. 'His sickness was protracted and complicated, confining him to his room during the greater portion of the last two years; but his robust physique patiently resisted the advances of [possibly dysentery] and it was only during the last four or five weeks that he was compelled to keep to his bed."

Illinois State Journal, May 24, 1867.

The Parish Register, St. Paul's Episcopal Church of Springfield, p. 327, MS., lists William S. Wallace, 67 [actually 65, he was born 1802 died in 1867} died of dropsy, buried Oak Ridge Cemetery.

Dr. Wallace's Service Record, National Archives, Washington, D. C. he died of disease contracted because of his overexposure during his tour of duty.

The funeral of Dr. Wallace took place at 3 p.m. on May 25, 1867 at St. Paul's Episcopal. *Illinois State Journal,* May 25, 1867.

When Dr. Wallace died the following children survived him:

Mary J. Baker
William F. Wallace
Frances Wallace
Edward D. Wallace
Charles E. Wallace

Probate Court Records, Sangamon County, Springfield, Illinois.

At the time of his death Dr. Wallace was still buying his drugs and medicines from Roland W. Diller. IBID Probate Court Records.

Following the death of Major Wallace, Frances applied for a pension and received one paying $25 per month, beginning on May 23, 1867. She listed her two children: Edward D. Wallace born September 14, 1852 and Charles N. Wallace born July 16, 1858. Pension File of Major William Smith Wallace, National Archives, Washington, D. C.

When Dr. Wallace died, Clark Moulton Smith, Sr [May 10, 1820-July 28, 1885] who was married to Ann Marie (Todd) Smith [1820-March 21, 1891] sister of Frances and Mary) became the administrater of his estate. On July 22, 1867 Frances Jane (Todd) waived her right to administer the estate of Dr. Wallace and asked Clark Moulton Smith, Sr.

Probate Court Records, Sangamon County, Springfield, Illinois.

Dr. Wallace left an estate of about $14, 500. IBId probate Court.

PHOTOGRAPHS, Etc.

Major Dr. William Smith Wallace

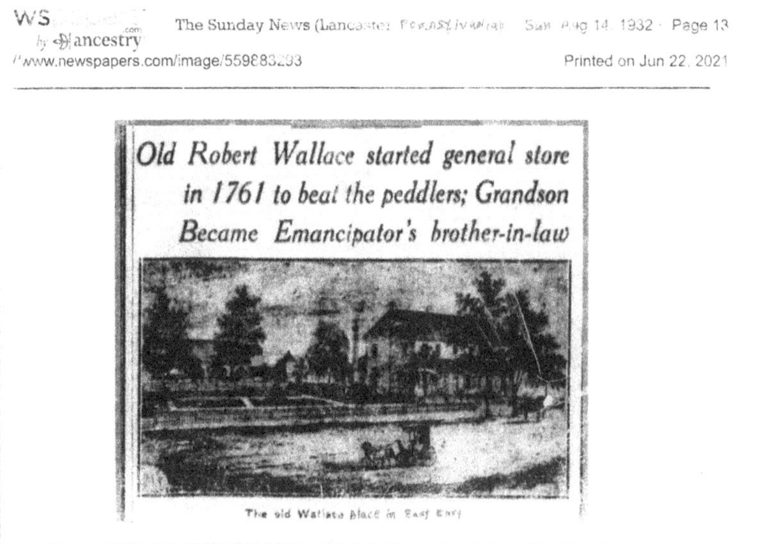

newspapers.com by ancestry — The Sunday News (Lancaster, Pennsylvania) · Sun, Aug 14, 1932 · Page 13

https://www.newspapers.com/image/559883293 — Printed on Jun 22, 2021

Old Robert Wallace started general store in 1761 to beat the peddlers; Grandson Became Emancipator's brother-in-law

The old Wallace place in East Earl

Wallace Home and Store

Lincoln and Dr. Wallace leaving for Washington

CLOSE FRIEND OF LINCOLN
IS DEAD IN SPRINGFIELD, ILL.

Roland W. Diller (1822–1905)
Close Friend of Lincoln and Wallace

Isaac Roland Diller II (1854–1943)
Friend and playmate of Tad and Willie Lincoln

Tombstone of Dr. Wallace,
Oakridge Cemetery, Springfield

Full hours and public access to the University Archives have resumed as of January 24, 2022. Appointments are required. Please consult our Special Procedures for Spring 2022 for details. X

Penn Libraries
University of Pennsylvania | University Archives & Records Center

Home » Online Exhibits » Penn History » Selected Lists of Medical Students, 1805-1860 » Surnames Beginning with "W"

PENN HISTORY

Selected Lists of Medical Students, 1805-1860

Surnames Beginning with "W"

These lists were compiled from hand-written ledgers by John C. Parker, Project Cataloger, College of Physicians. The information is drawn from three matriculation books located in the University Archives:

- **Medical Matriculation Book, 1806-January 4, 1816** (UPA 3 Pre-1820, document #1571)
- **Matriculation Book commenced 1816 ended 1834** (UPA 3 Pre-1820, document #1576)
- **Matriculation Book, Medical, 1834-1850** (UPC 2.7, document #12)

Key

- **year of attendance** indicates the final year of the academic year, i.e. 1825 refers to the 1824-1825 academic year
- **number enclosed in parentheses** after the year of attendance is a a simple sequential number assigned to each student for a particular academic year. The first student listed in the matriculation for a particular year is "1", the next is "2" and so on
- **$** indicates the matriculant earned the M.D. degree
- **d** indicates the matriculant died
- **co** and **nco** are believed to indicate commissioned and non-commissioned military officers

Selected List of Medical Students,
University of Pennsylvania Medical School, 1805–1860,
surnames beginning with "W"
University of Pennsylvania Archives and Record Center.

University of Pennsylvania
Medical Department Matriculants, 1806-1852
SURNAMES BEGINNING WITH
"W"

Wallace, John Gordon	Fredericksburg, VA	1848(319)	[d. 29 May [illegible]
		1849(428)	
		1850(47)$	
Wallace, James Brown	VA	1814(139)	
		1815(188)	
		1818$c.o.	
		1819(80)	
Wallace, James W. Dr.	?	1827(437)	
Wallace, James Westwood Mason	VA	1818(238)	[d. 5 Noven [illegible]
		1819(220)$	
Wallace, John Hooe?	VA	1813(149)	
		1815(216)$	
Wallace, John Young	NY	1827(406)	
		1831(303)$	
		1832(378)	
Wallace, Joseph	MD	1812(6)	
		1813(79)	
Wallace, Joshua Maddox	NJ	1835(224)	[d. 10 Nover [illegible]
		1836(278)$	
	Philadelphia	1837(349)	
Wallace, Michael	King George Co., VA	1843(102)	
Wallace, Robert M.	MD	1834(59)	
		1836(204)$	
	Dorchester, MD	1844(423)	
Wallace, Thomas F.	Marion, AL	1848(157)	
		1849(131)$	
Wallace, William	VA	1835(8)$	
Wallace, William D.	Cheraw, SC	1848(333)	
		1849(85)	
		1850(391)$	
Wallace, William M.	PA	1831(80)	
→ Wallace, William S.	PA	1822(203)	
		1823(193)	

U of P Medical Dept. Matriculants, 1806-1852: W
$ = received the M. D. degree
d = died

* Continued Next Page
No Wallace

William S. Wallace
dates attended Medical School 1821–1823

Full hours and public access to the University Archives have resumed as of January 24, 2022. Appointments are required. Please consult our Special Procedures for Spring 2022 for details. X

University of Pennsylvania
Medical Department Matriculants, 1806-1852
SURNAMES BEGINNING WITH
"W"

		1841(201)$	
Walker, Percy	AL	1835(64)$	[d. 31 December 1
Walker, Peter M.	Orange, NC	1840(174)	
Walker, Philip	PA	1818(329)	
Walker, Robert R.	?	1812$c.o.	
Walker, Thomas	PA	1822(227)	
Walker, Ths. L.	TN	1819(124)	
Walker, Thomas Lindsay	Albemarle Co., VA	1840(258)$	[d. Lynchburg, VA
		1841(379)	
Walker, Thomas R.	Amherst, VA	1850(347)$	[d. 1 October 1901
Walker, William	Greensboro, AL	1852(232)	
Walker, William	Nashville, TN	1842(78)	[A.B. 1838, U. Na:
		1843(56)$	
Walker, William A.	Sparta, GA	1850(313)	
Walker, William A.	TN	1831(312)	
Walker, William E.	Brunswick Co., VA	1845(65)	[d. 1869, Lynchbu
	Arents X-roads*, Greenville Co., VA	1846(390)$	
Walker, William P.	LA	1839(254)	
Walker, Wyatt P.	VA	1825(150)	
Wall, Alexander Alfred	Huntsville, AL	1848(60)	[d. 11 July 1904, T
		1849(36)$	
Wall, J. W.	Winchester, VA	1851(nco)	
Wall?, John	PA	1807(61)	
Wall, Richard Z. R.	NC	1833(127)	
		1834(122)$	
Wall, Robert Eldridge	Winchester, VA	1842(159)	[d. 15 December 1
		1843(43)$	
Wall, Thomas William Curlette	?	1851$c.o.	[d. 21 August 190
Wall, William M.	Caswell, NC	1841(4)	
		1843(214)	
Wallace, Caleb B.	KY	1808(123)$	
Wallace, Edward	PA	1835(164)	
		1836(33)$	
Wallace, Horace B.	Philadelphia	1836(102)	

U of P Medical Dept. Matriculants, 1806-1852: W

$ = received the M. D. degree

d. = died

Edward Wallace
dates attended Medical School 1834–1836

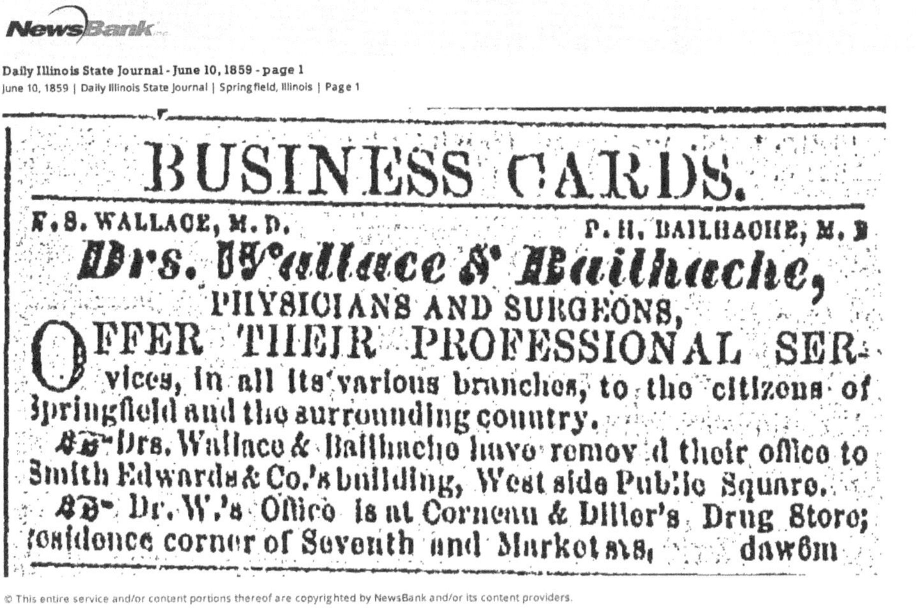

NewsBank

Daily Illinois State Journal - June 10, 1859 - page 1

June 10, 1859 | Daily Illinois State Journal | Springfield, Illinois | Page 1

BUSINESS CARDS.

F. S. WALLACE, M. D. P. H. BAILHACHE, M. D.

Drs. Wallace & Bailhache,

PHYSICIANS AND SURGEONS,

OFFER THEIR PROFESSIONAL SERvices, in all its various branches, to the citizens of Springfield and the surrounding country.

☞ Drs. Wallace & Bailhache have removed their office to Smith Edwards & Co.'s building, West side Public Square.

☞ Dr. W.'s Office is at Corneau & Diller's Drug Store; residence corner of Seventh and Market sts. daw6m

June 10, 1859 advertisement from Illinois State Daily Journal listing addresses of Drs. Wallace & Bailhache and Dr. Wallace's office at Corneau & Diller's Drugstore Courtesy of the Sangamon Valley Collection, Lincoln Library.

East side of Market St. (now Capitol) Corneau & Diller's Drugstore IBID Lincoln Library.

West side of Market St. Smith Edwards & Co. IBID, Lincoln Library.

BIBLIOGRAPHY

BOOKS, Websites, Articles, Etc.

Abraham Lincoln Papers at the Library of Congress.

Ancestry.com

Bailhache, Dr. Preston H., "Recollections of A Springfield Doctor," *Journal of the Illinois State Historical Society*, Spring 1954, Vol. 47, No. 1, pp. 57–63.

Baker, Jean H., *Mary Todd Lincoln: A Biography,* Chapter 4.

Basler, Roy P, (ed.), *Collected Works of Abraham Lincoln,* (CWAL), Vol. II, p. 45.

Basler, Roy P., (ed.), *Collected Works of Abraham Lincoln,* "A. Lincoln to Joshua F. Speed," Springfield, May 18, 1843.

Berry, Stephen, *House of Abraham: Lincoln & The Todds, A Family Divided by War, p.188.*

Burlingame, Michael, *Abraham Lincoln: A Life,* p. 826. 1855 Springfield Directory, 1855–56.

Civil War Pension File of Major William Smith Wallace, National Archives, Washington D. C.

Civil war Service Record of William Smith Wallace, National Archives, Washington, D. C. *Collected Works of Abraham Lincoln.*

FindAGrave.com

Hertz, Emanuel, (ed.), *Lincoln Talks,* Isaac R. Diller, NY, 1939, 74,

Hickey, James, "The Lincoln Account of The Corneau and Diller Drug Store 1849–1861," *Journal of the Illinois State Historical Society, Vol. 77,* Spring, 1984, p.60.

Houston, Frances R., Records of the Medical Alumni Society, University of Pennsylvania.

Keplinger, John. G., "In This Place and These People," *The Sunday News,* February 12, 1950.

Lehrman Institute, "Mr. Lincoln and Friends, The Politicians, William S. Wallace, 1802–1867.

Lincoln Papers at the Library of Congress.

Mearns, David C. (ed.), *The Lincoln Papers*, New York, 1948, II, 519, 1867. National Archives.

Probate Court Records, Sangamon County, Illinois, Springfield, 1867.

Records of the Medical Alumni Society, University of Pennsylvania. *Mary*

Report, Adjutant General State of Illinois, II, 118, VIII, 453.

Riddle, Donald W., *Congressman Abraham Lincoln,* Urbana, Illinois, 1957, p. 189.

Ringwalt, J. T., *The Diller Family*, privately printed, Philadelphia, 1877, 62. pgs.

Sandburg, Carl & Angle, Paul M., *Mary Lincoln,* "Mary Lincoln to Elizabeth Todd Grimsley;" p.208.

Sangamon County Courthouse, Springfield, Marriage Record II, 89.

St. Paul's Parish Register, II, St. Paul's Episcopal Church, Springfield, Illinois, Register Volume 1838–1905.

Seyfert, Hon. A. G., 'The Wallace Family and the Wallace Store of East Earl," *Journal of the Lancaster County Historical Society, Vol. 28, no. 2, 1925, no. 1.*

Springfield Census of 1860, Illinois State Archives.

Temple. Dr. Wayne C., "Loafing With Lincoln," *Lincoln Herald,* Summer 1961, Vol. 63, no. 2, p. 55–62.

Thornbahn, H. Clifton, "History of the Wallace Clan: Robert Wallace Opened General Store In East Earl, Twp.," *The Sunday News, August 14, 1932, P. 13.*

United States Official Register, 1861, 62, William S. Wallace To A. Lincoln," Springfield, Illinois, April 11, 1861, R. T. L. Collection. *University of Pennsylvania Archives & Records Center*

Wilson, Douglas I. & Rodney O. Davis, (eds.), *Herndon' s Informants: letters, Interviews and Statements About Abraham Lincoln,* p.485.

NEWSPAPERS

Illinois Daily Journal

Illinois State Journal

New York Tribune

Sangamo Journal (Springfield, Illinois)

Springfield Gazette

Sunday News (Lancaster Pennsylvania)

Sunday Times-Herald (Chicago)

PERIODICALS

American Druggist and Pharmaceutical Record

Journal of the Illinois State Historical Society

Journal of the Lancaster County Historical Society (PA)

Lincoln Herald

PHOTOGRAPHS, Etc.

Major Dr. William Smith Wallace, FindAGrave.com (FRONT COVER)

Wallace Home and Store, East Earl, Lancaster County, PA., *Sunday* News, Lancaster, PA

Frances (Todd) Wallace, FindAGrave.com

Lincoln and Dr. Wallace leaving for Washington February 11, 1861 Google Images

Roland W. Diller (1822–1905) Close Friend of Lincoln and Wallace, from Lancaster County, Pa. Google Images

Isaac Roland Diller II (1854–1943) Friend and playmate of Tad and Willie Lincoln; his father Isaac Roland Diller also from Lancaster County Google Images.

Tombstone of Dr, Wallace, Oakridge Cemetery, Springfield, FindAGrave.com

Selected List of Medical Students, University of Pennsylvania Medical School, 1805–1860, surnames beginning with "W". University of Pennsylvania Archives and Record Center.

William S. Wallace dates attended Medical School 1821–1823. IBID Record Center.

Edward Wallace dates attended Medical School 1834–1836. IBID Record Center.

June 10, 1859 advertisement from Illinois State Daily Journal listing addresses of Drs. Wallace & Bailhache and Dr. Wallace's office at Corneau & Diller's Drugstore Courtesy of the Sangamon Vallery Collection, Lincoln Library.

East side of Market St. (now Capitol) Corneau & Diller's Drugstore IBID Lincoln Library.

West side of Market St. Smith Edwards & Co. IBID, Lincoln Library.

ABOUT THE AUTHOR

The author, Donald Motier, dressed in a replica uniform of his great-grandfather, Sgt. Charles Powers' grave Greenwood Cemetery, Lancaster, PA Nov. 9, 2008

Donald Motier is the author of over 20 books including poetry, historical fiction, novellas, biographies and travel. *Lincoln's Physician, a Biography of Dr. William Smith Wallace* was inspired by Dr. Wayne C. Temple, retired Deputy Archivist of the Illinois State Archives and leading living authority on the life and family of Abraham Lincoln and is the author of many scholarly works.

Donald Motier has written three previous books on Lincoln and his family: *Mystic Chords of Memory: The Lost Journal of William Wallace Lincoln (2009), Saving Lincoln: Mystic Chords of Memory Part 2 (2014) and He Had Rare Lights: A Biography of William* Wallace Lincoln (2019). He lives and writes in Pennsylvania.

CPSIA information can be obtained
at www.ICGtesting.com
Printed in the USA
LVHW071914191222
735554LV00018B/772

9 781959 450979